Meet ... everyone from

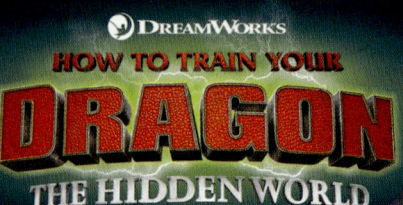

Hiccup is the young chief of Berk. Hiccup fell off a dragon when he was a boy and he has a prosthetic foot.

Astrid

Stormfly

Hiccup

Astrid is Hiccup's girlfriend. Her dragon is **Stormfly**.

tail fin

Toothless

Toothless is a Night Fury. He's the Alpha – the chief of all the dragons. Hiccup made a new tail fin for him. Toothless can't fly without Hiccup's help.

prosthetic foot

Snotlout is one of Hiccup's friends.

Valka is Hiccup's mother.

Hiccup and his friends live on the island of **Berk**. The Berkians love their dragons.

Grimmel is a famous dragon trapper. He is clever and dangerous. He wants to trap every Night Fury.

Grimmel

The trappers take dragons and put them in cages.

The Hidden World is the home of all dragons. Where is it? No one from Berk knows.

Before you read ...
What do you think? Can Hiccup find the Hidden World?

New Words

What do these new words mean? Ask your teacher or use your dictionary.

chief

Everyone listened to the **chief**.

arrow

She's got three **arrows**.

island

They lived on a small **island**.

cage

It's in a **cage**.

tail

This cat has a long **tail**.

take off

wings

They all have **wings**.

trap

It's a **trap**.

without

waterfall

It's a beautiful **waterfall**.

'Watch out!

What does the title *The Hidden World* mean? Ask your teacher.

Verbs

Present	Past
fall	fell
fly	flew
take	took

CHAPTER ONE
Only a boy

It was a dark night. Hiccup and his friends flew on their dragons. They flew to the trappers' island. Quietly, they opened the dragon cages.

A trapper saw them. 'Stop!' he shouted.
'Let's go!' said Hiccup.
Hiccup and Toothless flew away. The trappers' dragons flew after Toothless, their Alpha.
But no one saw the white dragon in her cage.

The new dragons came to Berk.

'This is your home now,' Hiccup said. 'There are no cages here.'

The dragons were happy, but there was a problem.

'Berk is our home,' said Astrid. 'But it's dangerous now. The trappers know that we're here.'

Not far away, the trappers talked to Grimmel.

'Bring the Night Fury here,' they said. 'The other dragons always come after him.'

'That's going to be easy!' laughed Grimmel. 'Hiccup is Berk's chief, and he's only a boy. And we have the white dragon.'

CHAPTER TWO
The Light Fury

Toothless looked at the white dragon. She was beautiful.

But when the white dragon saw Hiccup and Astrid, she flew away. Toothless could not fly after her.

'She was like Toothless,' said Hiccup. 'A Night Fury, but white.'

'A Light Fury,' said Astrid.

The next day, Toothless and Hiccup went back to the same place. The Light Fury wasn't there.

But Hiccup found an arrow.

'Oh no! Trappers!' said Hiccup. 'Watch out, Toothless!'

Toothless jumped back. A big trap closed in front of him.

'He's OK this time,' thought Hiccup. 'But the trappers are going to come back.'

That night, Grimmel walked quietly into Hiccup's home. 'I'm going to trap your Night Fury,' he said.

Suddenly Hiccup's friends were all around Grimmel. 'Now you're in *our* trap!' said Hiccup.

But Grimmel laughed. 'You're only a boy. You're nothing without your dragon,' he said. 'And next time, you're going to give your dragon to me.'

Hiccup talked to all the Berkians. 'Grimmel is too dangerous – for our dragons, and for us. Maybe we can all live happily in the Hidden World. My father sometimes talked about it. It's the home of the dragons, under a waterfall at the end of the world.'

'We can't live away from Berk!' said Snotlout angrily. 'Berk is our home!'

'But Berk is more than this place,' said Hiccup. '*We* are Berk – our people and our dragons.'

In the morning, they all said goodbye to their island and flew away.

CHAPTER THREE
A new home

After a long day, the Berkians came to a beautiful island.

'Let's stay here for now,' said Hiccup.

'OK,' said Valka. 'But where's Grimmel? I'm going to see.' She flew away on her dragon.

Hiccup made a better tail fin for Toothless.

'Now you can fly without me,' he said.

Toothless was very happy. He flew away to look for the Light Fury.

When he found her, they flew up and up. It was a dragon dance of love.

They came to a waterfall. The Light Fury flew into it, and Toothless went with her.

Valka came back to the new island. 'Grimmel and his men are going to be here tomorrow!' she said.

Everyone was frightened. 'Toothless isn't here, so the dragons have no Alpha. What are we going to do?' they asked Hiccup.

'I don't know,' said Hiccup.

'We need a better chief,' said Snotlout.

'Maybe Grimmel's right,' Hiccup said to Astrid. 'I'm nothing without Toothless.'
'Let's look for him,' said Astrid.
Stormfly flew Hiccup and Astrid far out to sea.
'Where's Stormfly going?' Hiccup asked.
'Look!' said Astrid. 'A waterfall …'
'… at the end of the world!' said Hiccup.

CHAPTER FOUR
The Hidden World

Stormfly flew down and down, into the Hidden World. There were lights of every colour.

'Wow! It's beautiful!' said Hiccup.

They saw hundreds of dragons.

'Look!' shouted Astrid. 'It's Toothless!'

Hiccup and Astrid got off Stormfly and watched. Toothless and the Light Fury were there in the Hidden World, and all the other dragons loved them.

'Let's go,' said Hiccup sadly. 'Toothless is happy here. He doesn't need us.'

But a big dragon saw them.

'Oh no!' shouted Hiccup.

Hiccup and Astrid ran. Now there were angry dragons everywhere.

Suddenly Toothless was there. He took Hiccup and Astrid in his feet.

'Thank you, Toothless!' said Hiccup.

They flew back to the new island with the Light Fury behind them.

But Hiccup saw something. 'Watch out!' he shouted.

An arrow went into the Light Fury and she fell.

'Grimmel's here!' said Astrid.

There was a second arrow, and Toothless fell too.

'Thank you for your Night Fury!' Grimmel shouted to Hiccup.

The trappers took Toothless and the Light Fury away. The other dragons could not help them, but they flew after their Alpha.

'What can we do?' Hiccup asked Astrid sadly.

'When things are bad, what do you always do?' she asked.

'Have a bad idea!' said Hiccup.

Hiccup made wings for his friends. 'We can fly to the trappers,' he said.

His friends were frightened. 'That's a very bad idea,' they said.

Hiccup jumped and opened his wings.

His friends jumped too. 'We can fly!' they shouted.

CHAPTER FIVE
A better place

Grimmel laughed. 'Now I have the Night Fury!' he said.

'Watch out!' shouted a trapper.

Suddenly Hiccup flew into Grimmel. Hiccup's friends were behind him.

'Open the cages!' shouted Astrid.

Grimmel flew away on the Light Fury. Hiccup and Toothless flew after them. They went up and up. The Light Fury was only a metre away …

'No!' shouted Hiccup. One of Grimmel's arrows went into Toothless and he started to fall.

Quickly, Hiccup jumped onto the Light Fury. Grimmel fell off, but he had a hand on Hiccup's prosthetic foot.

'I've got you!' Grimmel shouted. 'If I fall, you fall too!'

Hiccup thought quickly. 'Help Toothless!' he said to the Light Fury. He fell off her and she flew to Toothless.

Hiccup and Grimmel fell down and down.

'This is the end,' thought Hiccup.

But then he saw the Light Fury again. 'She's coming back for me!' he thought.

Hiccup had an idea. 'You haven't got me,' he said to Grimmel.

He took off his prosthetic foot. It fell into the sea – and Grimmel fell with it.

But Hiccup, in the Light Fury's arms, was OK.

'We did it!' shouted the Berkians. 'You're a great chief, Hiccup!'

But Toothless looked unhappily out to sea.

'I know,' said Hiccup. 'You need to take your dragons to the Hidden World. It's too dangerous here.'

Sadly, the Berkians and their dragons said goodbye.

Toothless looked at Hiccup. His eyes were big and sad.

'I love you too,' said Hiccup. 'Now, go.'

The Berkians watched as Toothless and all the dragons flew away to the Hidden World.

'They can come back,' said Hiccup, 'when our world is a better place for dragons.'

THE END

Real World

HIDDEN WORLDS

There are problems for many animals in our world today. But the animals in these hidden worlds can live happily.

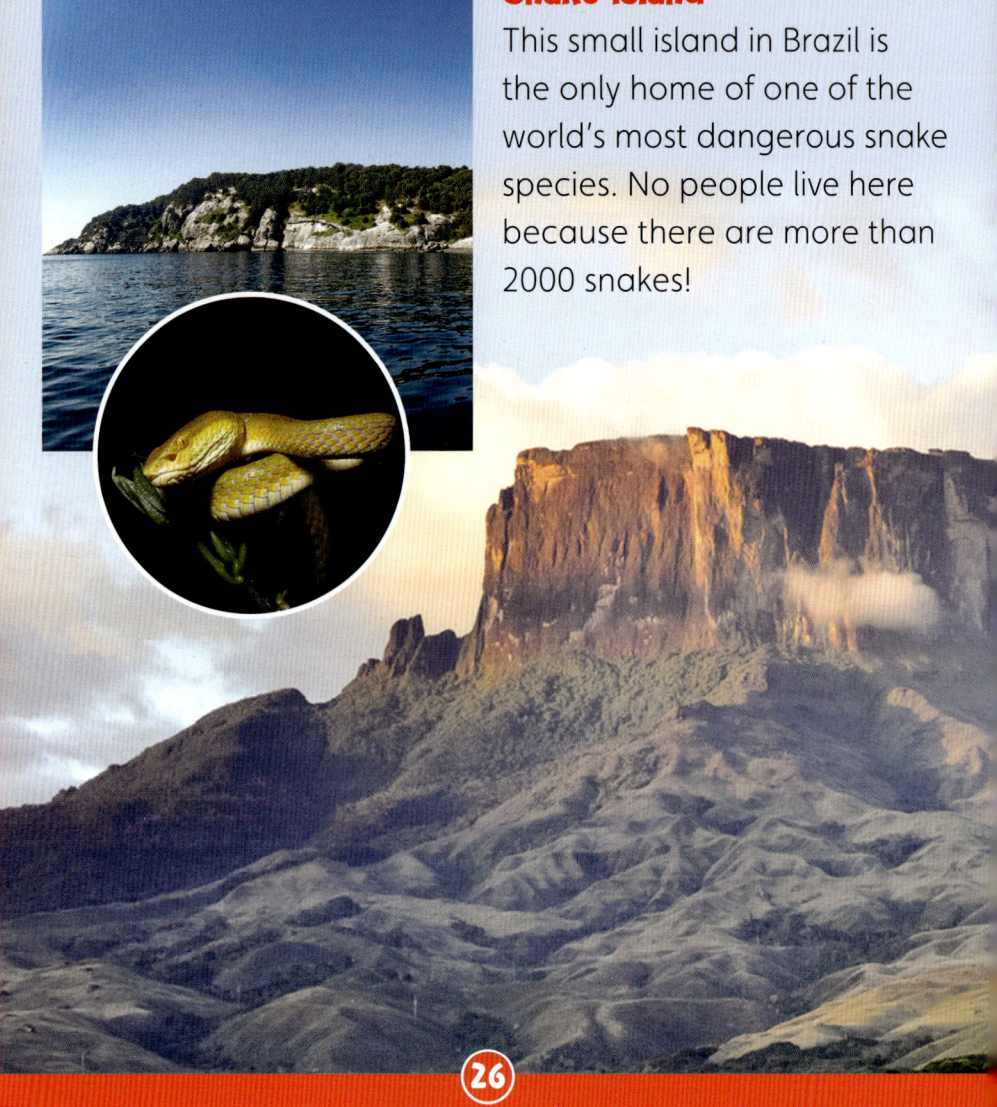

Snake Island

Snake island

This small island in Brazil is the only home of one of the world's most dangerous snake species. No people live here because there are more than 2000 snakes!

Mount Bosavi volcano

Would you like to go to these hidden worlds? Why? / Why not?

Rat volcano

At the top of this old volcano in Papua New Guinea, you can go down one kilometre to a hidden world. Some species live only here. One species is a rat. It's about 82 cm long. That's bigger than a cat!

Toad mountain

It's not easy to climb the tepui mountains in South America. Most of the species there live only on one or two mountains. This toad is one of them. It can't jump far. When it sees something dangerous, it rolls away like a ball.

What do these words mean? Find out.
species   volcano   climb   mountain   roll

A tepui mountain in South America

After you read

1 Match to make sentences.

a) Grimmel   i) helped Toothless when he fell.
b) Toothless   ii) is the chief of Berk.
c) Hiccup   iii) went with Hiccup to the Hidden World.
d) Snotlout   iv) wanted to trap Toothless.
e) Astrid   v) wanted a better chief for Berk.
f) The Light Fury   vi) is the dragon Alpha.

2 True (✓) or False (✗)? Write in the box.

a) The trappers had a white dragon in a cage. ✓
b) The dragons on Berk lived in small cages. ☐
c) The Berkians could not stay on Berk. ☐
d) Hiccup made a new tail fin for Toothless. ☐
e) Toothless was frightened of the Light Fury. ☐
f) Hiccup and Astrid made friends with all of the dragons in the Hidden World. ☐
g) The Berkians went to live with the dragons in the Hidden World. ☐

Where's the popcorn?
Look in your book.
Can you find it?

Puzzle time!

1 Look at pages 4–5. Write the words and find the name of Snotlout's dragon.

2 What's different? Circle the odd word out.

a) tail   legs   wings   (cage)
b) home   trapper   girlfriend   chief
c) sea   island   foot   waterfall
d) jump   fly   arrow   help

3 How can Toothless go to the Light Fury? Read and follow.

First, Toothless must find the island.
Then he must go through the waterfall.
He must stay away from the traps.
He can't go near the arrows.

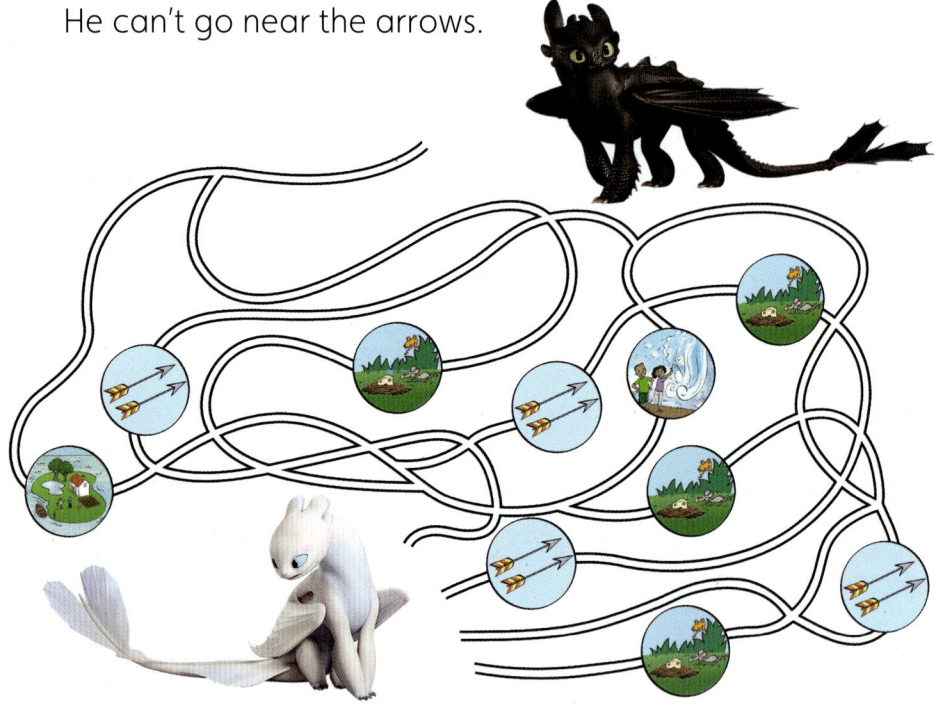

4 Read and (✓). Then ask your friends.

Would you like to: Yes   No

a) be friends with a dragon? ✓

b) live on a small island?

c) have wings and fly?

d) have a tail?

e) be a chief?

Imagine...

In small groups, mime a scene from the story. Then ask your friends some questions.

Who were we?

You were Toothless and Hiccup.

What did we do?

Hiccup found an arrow and shouted at Toothless. Toothless stopped. Then a trap closed.

What did we say?

Hiccup said, 'Watch out, Toothless!'

Chant

1 Listen and read.

Dragons, you must go!

Dragons, you must go.
Berk is now too small
And trappers know the place.
They want to trap you all.

Dragons, you must go
Far, far out to sea
To find the waterfall.
You can't stay here with me.

Dragons, you must go.
Say goodbye today!
The Hidden World's your home,
So dragons, fly away!

2 Say the chant.